This booklet is the second in a series covering feltmaking techniques. It deals with the making of seamless hollow forms for functional items such as hats and bags but also for sculpting into decorative shapes. It is the type of feltmaking used extensively by Scandinavian feltmakers for hats, bags, mittens and boots and involves making felt in a three dimensional seamless form. The success of this technique depends on confident handling of the fibres and calls for rather more skill than is required for making flat pieces so it is advisable for the feltmaker to have some experience before tackling this method.

Making hollow seamless felt requires the use of a resist template which will be covered all over with wool fibres and will prevent the layers of fibres from felting together. Templates may be made from cardboard, cloth or plastic. If using cardboard, firm packing-cartons are ideal and after cutting the template the edges can be reinforced by covering with sticky parcel-tape. Avoid using card with a decorative surface such as mounting board as this surface will transfer itself to the wool fibres during felting. If cloth is chosen it needs to be firm and closely woven. It is easy to wet out the fibres using a cloth template but it can adhere to the fibres during felting unless great care is taken. Plastic templates are easier to use if the plastic is of a heavy weight as the edges can be followed when building up the shape and such templates also have the advantage of being re-useable. The plastic used by builders for laying under concrete is ideal and heavy weights of plastic sheeting can also be purchased at garden centres. Bubble plastic with small bubbles is suitable and thin vinyl floor covering makes excellent hardwearing templates for footwear. When making the templates allowance for shrinkage must be added to the planned size of the project.

Once the all important techniques of calculating measurements and making the templates have been mastered then the fun of designing and making innovative shapes can begin.

Making Templates

Bags are an ideal first project for three dimensional feltmaking and can be made in a wide variety of shapes and sizes. For a first project avoid a shape which is too small and fiddly and avoid being over ambitious and tackling a shape which is too large. A good size to begin with would be approximately 24 cm wide and 20 cm deep with a 10 cm flap. Experiment with different shapes and sizes, cutting out shapes in paper until you find the design you like, measure this and make a template. The average allowance for shrinkage in this type of feltmaking is 40%.

Template for a bag finished size 24cm x 20 cm + 10cm flap over

Calculating template size:

Take the original measurements of width and depth and add 40%. (do each one separately)

An easy way to calculate this:
Original measurement x $\frac{4}{10}$ = the extra required for shrinkage.

So original measurement + shrinkage allowance = size of template

Diagram 1 - size and shape of planned bag with flap folded over.

Diagram 2 - paper pattern made to size of finished bag with flap extended (template needs to include the flap).

Diagram 3 - template which includes 40% allowance for shrinkage for both bag and flap.

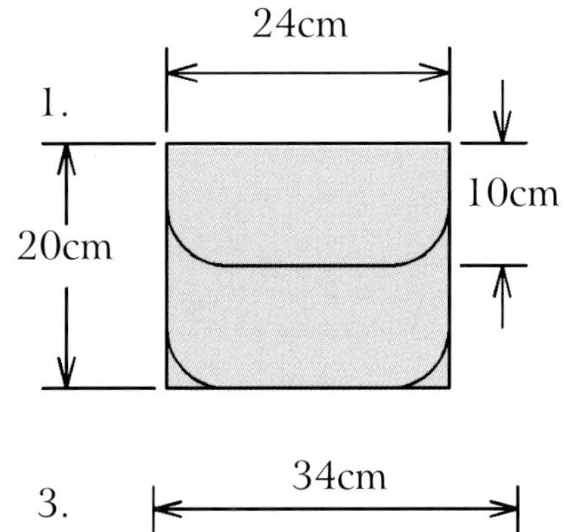

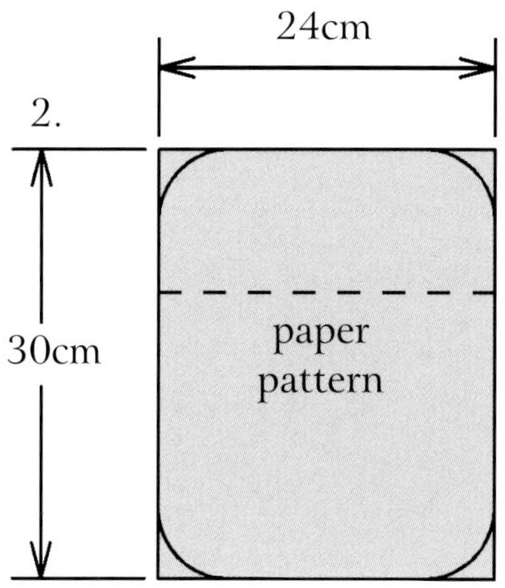

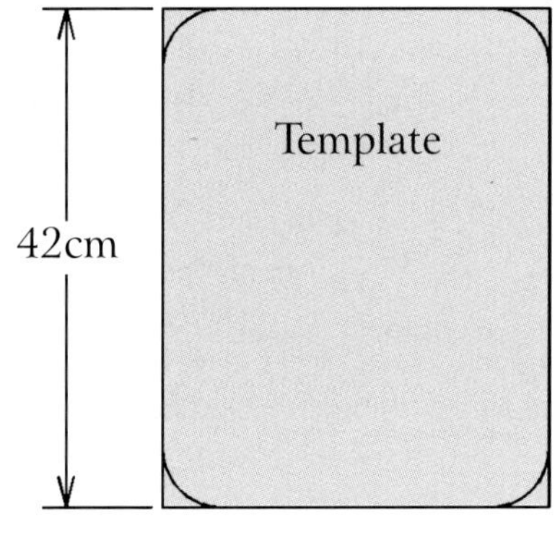

To make a simple seamless bag

Choice of fibre
The fibre should be chosen to suit the purpose of the planned bag e.g. small decorative bags and purses can be made from Merino while larger bags intended for harder wear require a harder wearing wool e.g. Icelandic, Finn Wool, Gotland or Blue Faced Leicester

Equipment:

Old towels
Bamboo / matchstick mat
Bubble wrap plastic (small bubbles)
Length of heavy wooden dowelling or broom handle
Net
Plastic bottle with small holes drilled in the lid
Plastic jug
Waterproof apron
Rubber gloves
Plastic carrier bag - lightweight supermarket type.
Merino wool tops
Soap

Method:

1. Lay out folded towel with bamboo blind on top then bubble plastic on top of bamboo blind.
2. Lay plastic template on bubble plastic.
3. Pull out small lengths of combed tops and lay these pieces around the edge with half the length overlapping the edge of the template like a fringe as in *diagram (a)*
4. Continue to pull out lengths of fibre in this way and fill in the shape of the pattern with overlapping layers in the same way as you would for a flat piece *see diagram (b)*
5. Place a second layer of overlapping fibres at right angles to the first one but this time the fibres should only reach the edge of the template *see diagram (c)*

a *b* *c*

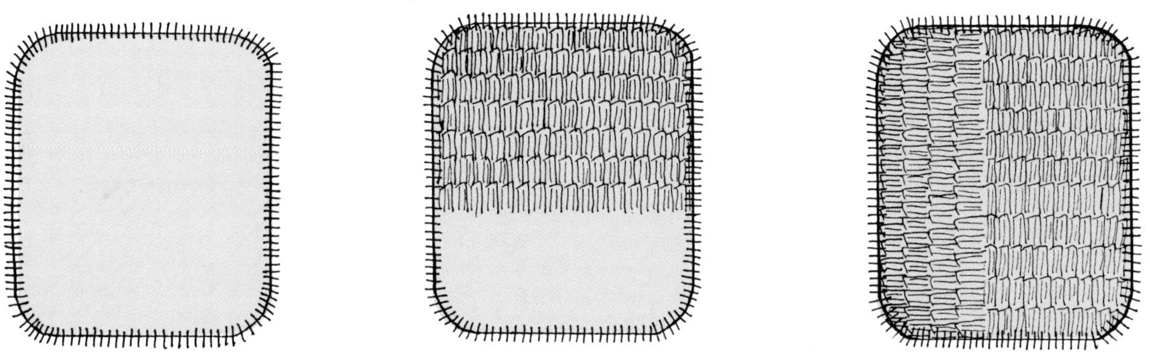

cover edge of template — layer 1 — layer 2

6. Cover fibres with a piece of net and **carefully** pour warm soapy water in to the centre of the fibres taking care not to disturb the layers. Gently press the fibres with a pad made by folding a plastic carrier bag so that the water is absorbed, work from the centre gradually pushing the water outwards but trying to keep the fringe dry.

7. Remove net carefully, lift the template and fibres and turn over so that the template is on top.
8. Turn the overlapping fibres back over the edge of the template *see diagram (d)*
9. Put one layer of overlapping fibres on top of the template until it is covered, this layer should lie in the same direction as the **first** layer of side one *see diagram (e)*
10. Lay a second layer of overlapping fibres at right angles to the first layer allowing the fibres to overlap the template *see diagram (f)*

d

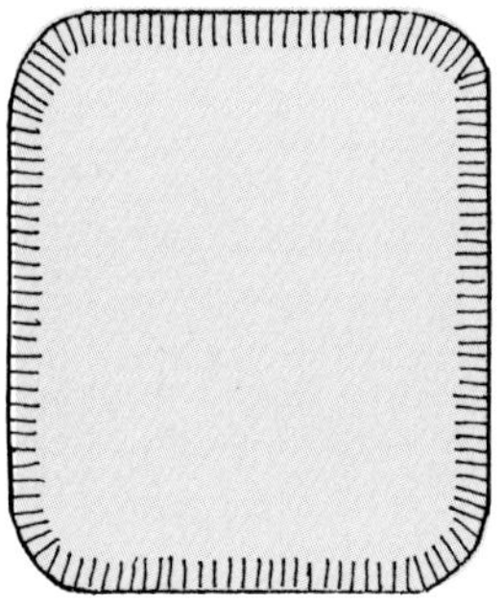

side 2 turn fringe over edge

e

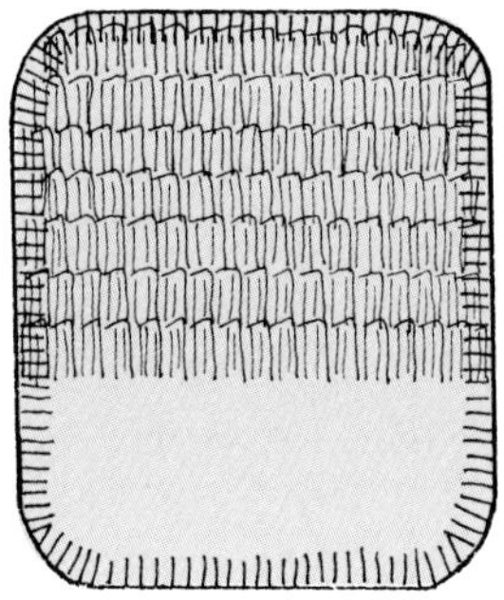

side 2 layer 1

f

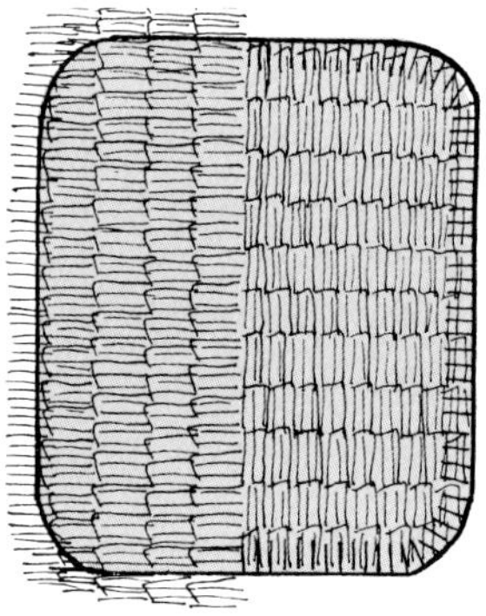

side 2 layer 2

11. Place net in position, wet these fibres and press the water through until all layers are wet.
12. Turn fibres and template over, turn the overlapping fibres back over the edge so that the resulting package is the same size as the template.
13. Lay out a fringe and add a third layer of overlapping fibres at right angles to the last one, place net on top and wet.
14. Remove net, turn package and fold over any overlapping edges.
15. Add third layer of fibre to the second side (no fringe required) wet and tuck in any edges.
16. Cover fibres with net and gently rub over the surface, rubbing from the edges inwards to keep the package exactly the size of the template.
17. Turn package over, cover with net and repeat the rubbing process.
18. Remove net and add any decoration rubbing gently with soap to get it to adhere to the wool fibres. Rub around the edges of the package to ensure that it retains its shape.
19. Gently roll the package up in bubble wrap and bamboo blind using a dowel to keep the roll flat.
20. Roll gently approximately 50 times, open up, turn package over and repeat.
21. Continue in this way until the fibres begin to harden but take care not to form a hard seam around the edge. Rolling should be done alternately across the width and then along the length of the package to keep it even.
22. When fibres have hardened sufficiently to handle or the template begins to curl, carefully cut the fibres along the top of the package and remove template *see diagram (g)*

(g)

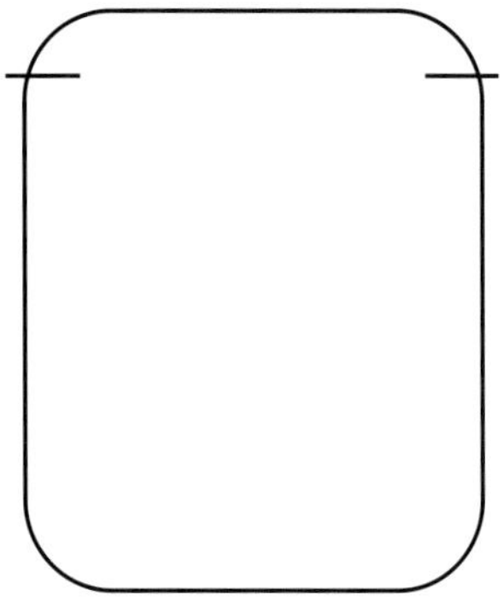

slit top edge between a and b

(h)

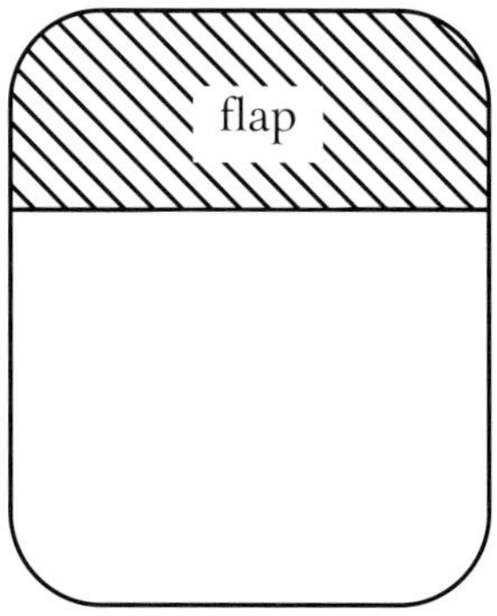

cut away one layer on underside of flap

23. Carefully place one hand inside the package and with the other hand gently rub around the fold on the outside to avoid having a ridge.
24 Re-roll in mat without the dowelling or bubble plastic for 30 / 40 times, open up to ensure that the two sides of the bag are not felting together. Turn over and repeat.

Hardening is continued in this way gradually adding hot water to the roll and increasing the pressure. The bag must also be turned inside out so that both sides of the felt are hardened. When the felt is quite firm the flap should be cut to shape so that the cut edges will be felted as the rolling continues. When hardening is complete, rinse and spin out excess water, pull into shape and allow to dry.

Felted Footwear

Seamless slippers and boots are also made three dimensionally around a resist template. The template must be made to fit the required shoe size plus allowance for shrinkage. This may be done by taking the measurements directly from the foot or by using a last.

Making a boot template using the foot as a guide:

1. Stand barefoot (or with socks but no shoes) on a large piece of paper and draw around the outline of the foot.
2. Mark the centre point between heel and toe.
3. Draw a vertical line from the heel and one from the mid-point to form the leg of the boot.
4. Draw a horizontal line to form the top of the boot.
5. The length of the leg can be varied according to choice. A short leg is easier to handle to start with.
6. Measure out 5 cm from the shape and draw in the new outline - this is to allow for shrinkage.
7. Cut out the enlarged shape from paper.
8. Use this pattern to cut out two identical templates from heavy plastic or cut a template for both boots joined across the top of the leg. This allows both boots to be laid out at once ensuring that the same amount of fibre is used for each boot.

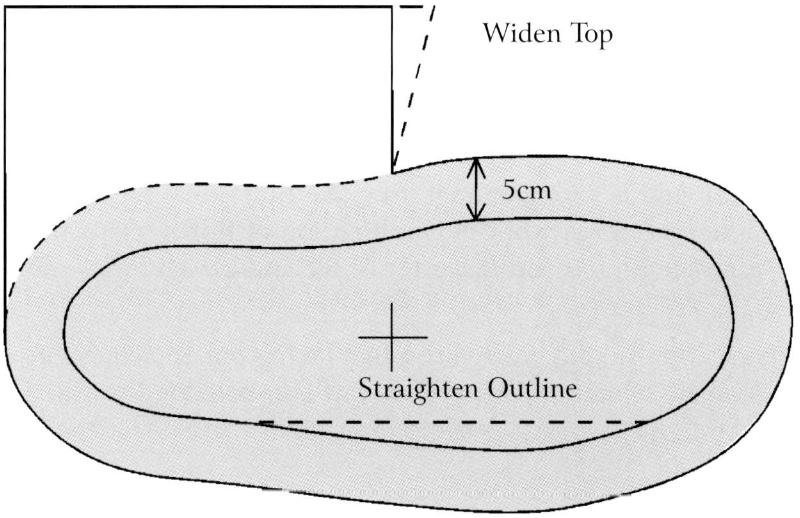

Polystyrene lasts are now available in sizes from birth up to size 10 and make it much easier to make footwear which fits. When making a template for use with the lasts then take the measurement from the last rather than the foot.

To work out the size for the template when using lasts :

1. Lay the shoe last side down on a sheet of paper and draw around the outline.
2. Measure out 5 cm from the shape and draw in the new outline - this is to allow for shrinkage.
3. If making a pattern for boots then extend the leg to the desired size.
4. Cut out the enlarged shape from paper.
5. Use this pattern to cut out two identical templates from heavy plastic or cut a template where the two shapes are joined together along the top of the leg. This allows both boots to be laid out together ensuring that the same amount of fibre is used for each boot.

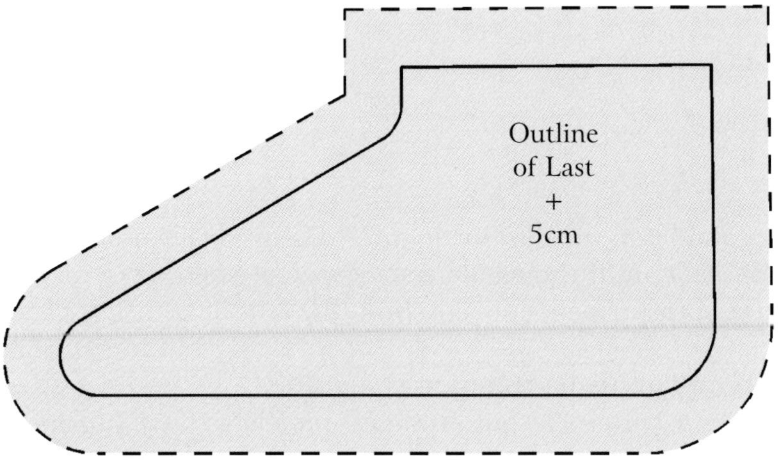

Preparing the lasts :

1. Cover each last tightly with cling film which will protect it during use.
2. Place each last inside a lightweight plastic bag (sandwich or freezer type) - this gives something to pull on when finally removing the felt boot from the last.

Felted Footwear - useful tips

Templates

Make the template from something which is strong enough and thick enough to feel the edges through the fibre so that you can lay the fibres out accurately but still be able to roll it e.g. vinyl flooring.

Fibres

Use a fibre which felts well and is strong enough to make functional footwear e.g. Icelandic, Blue Faced Leicester, Gotland or Finn wool. A combination of fibres seems to give a very satisfactory result for example Blue Faced Leicester or Icelandic with Finn wool works well.

Laying out fibres

Use at least five layers of fibres taking great care when laying out to achieve even layers and good joins at the edges of the template. Extra fibres can also be added to the lower part of the foot for strength.

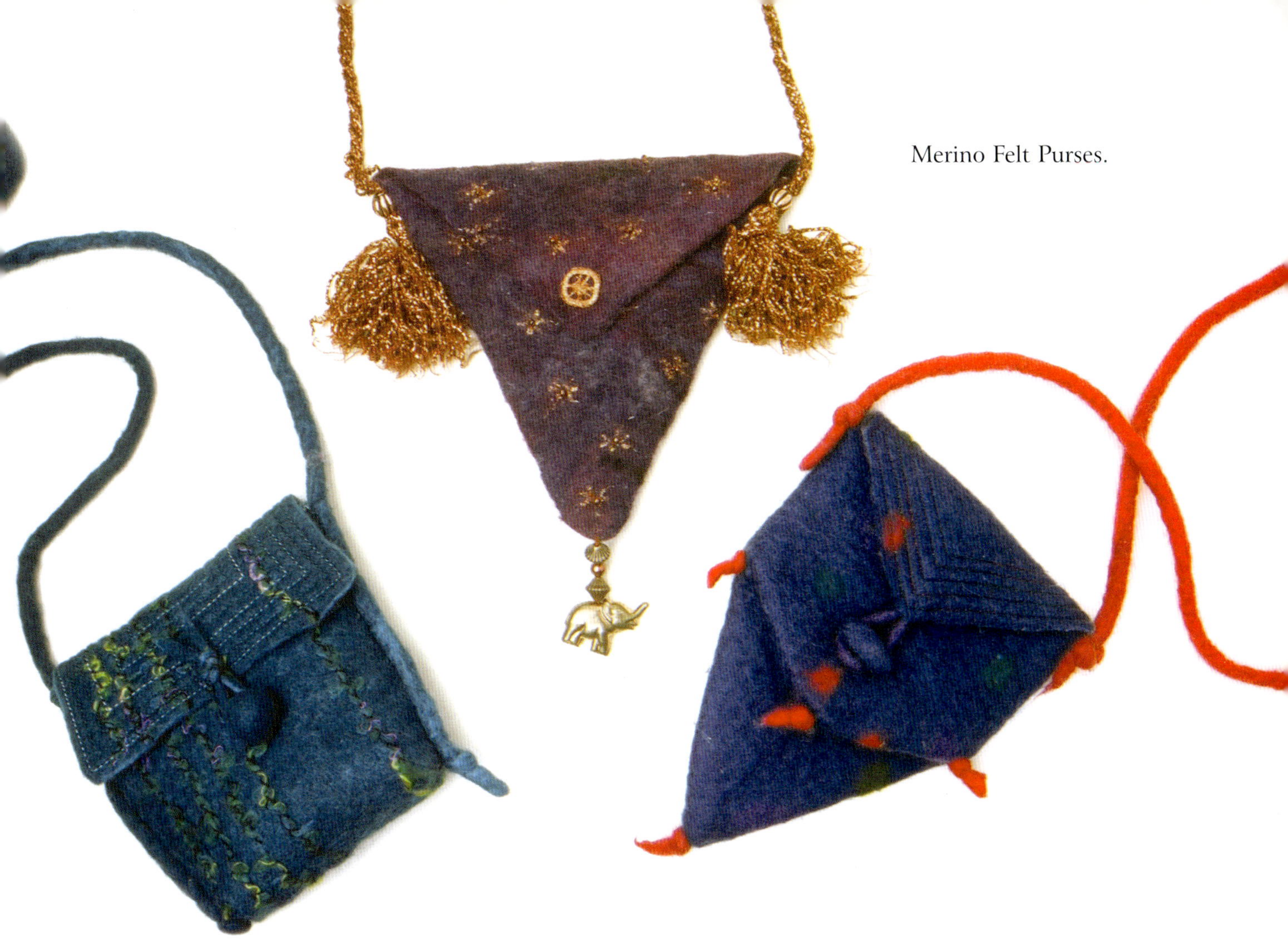

Merino Felt Purses.

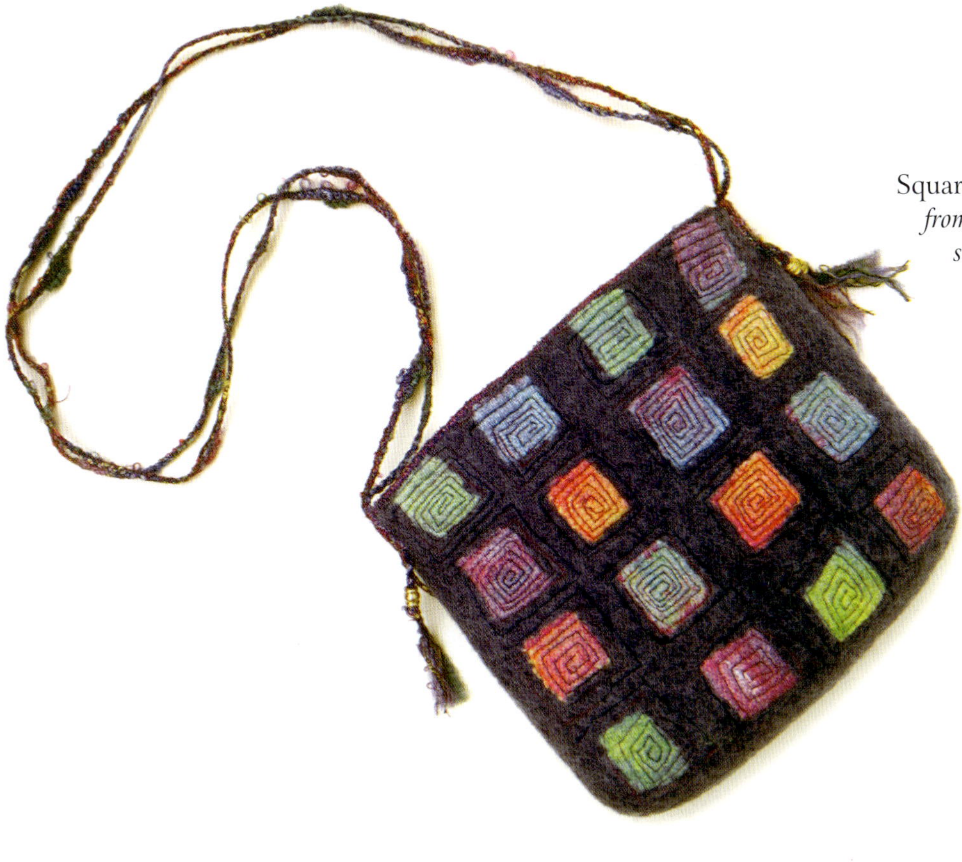

Squares - *shaped and moulded bag from Merino and Finn wool with silk paper squares felted on the surface. Finished with free machine stitching and decorative cord straps.*

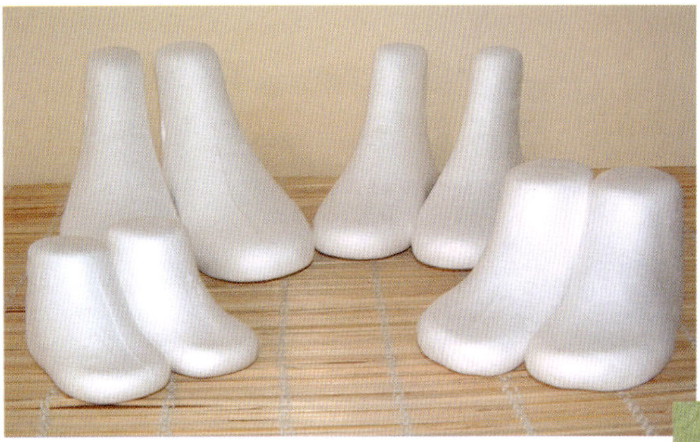

Polystyrene lasts available in a wide range of sizes from child to adult make it much easier to shape felt footwear.

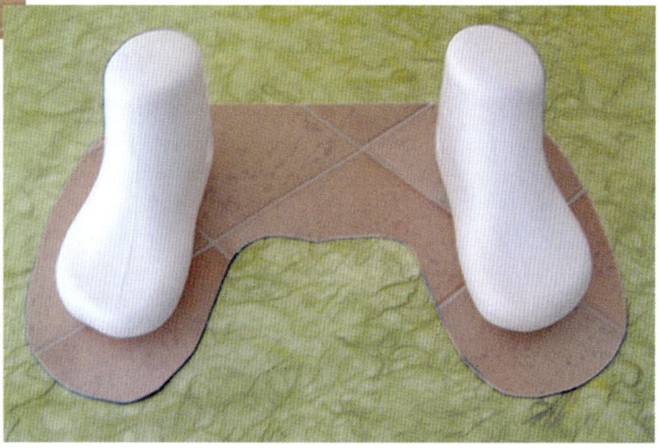

Polystyrene lasts and the template required for footwear to fit them.

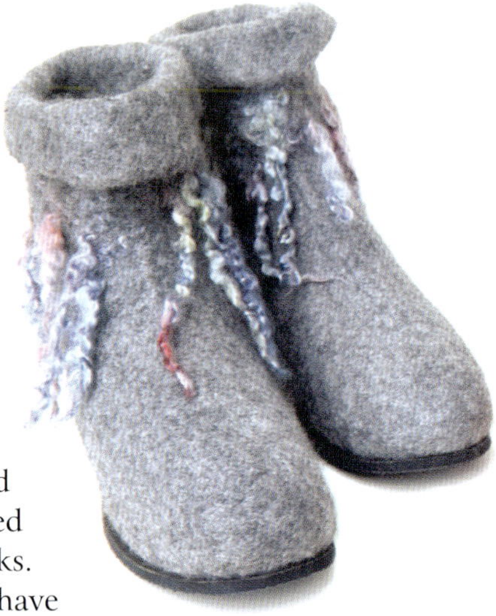

Grey Gotland boots decorated with dyed Wensleydale locks. These boots have been professionally soled and heeled to prolong wear.

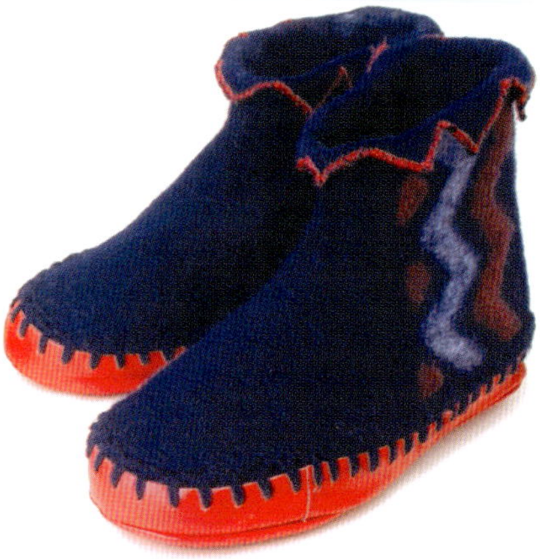

Navy Merino Boots with pre-felted inlay design on legs. Leather soles hand stitched in place.

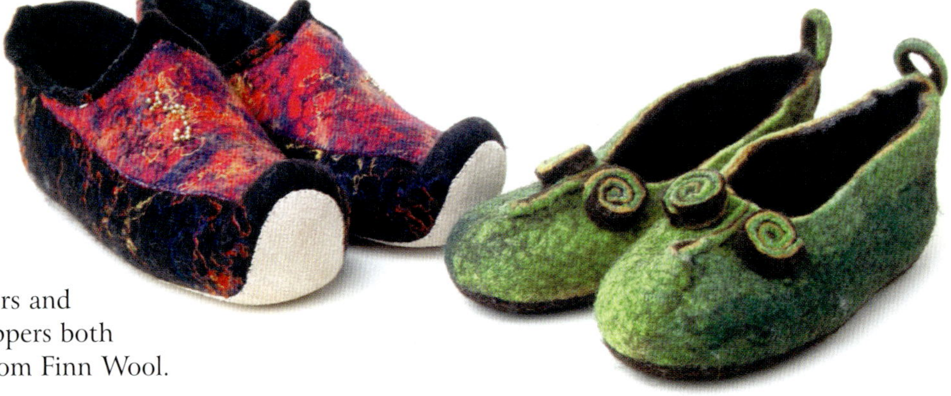

Ali Baba Slippers and Ballerina Slippers both made from Finn Wool.

Suggested method for laying out fibres :

1. Make a fringe of fibre overlapping the edge of the template on the first layer.
2. Second layer at right angles to the first but no fringe.
3. Wet out fibre, keeping fringe as dry as possible and turn template over.
4. Turn fringe back over edge of template and gently flatten down.
5. Repeat stages 1 - 4 on second side of template.
6. Layers 3 & 4 are laid down in the same way as layers 1& 2 on both sides.
7. Before starting on layer 5 ensure that all the fibres are lying flat and turning accurately over the template with no loose edges.
8. Layer 5 has a fringe and is then wet out and turned over.
9. Layer 5 on the other side has no fringe just fill in with fibre up to the fringe.

The above is a little long winded so to paraphrase - *use five layers of fibre, layer 1 & 3 on each side have fringes and layer 5 has fringe on one side only. So five layers in total and five fringes/*

10. Wetting out and hardening are carried out as for the bag instructions on page 4.

Before starting to roll spend time rubbing the edges to firm them up to prevent them from spreading when rolling begins.

Shaping the felt boots

Work with the felt boot/slipper rolling it until it has shrunk down almost to the required size and then place it on the last. Continue shrinking by rubbing the felt directly on to the last and using hot water until a close fit is achieved. Trim thc top of the boot/slipper to the required shape and place the boot (still on the last) into a sock or leg of a pair of tights and knot tightly against the top of the boot. Place in a washing machine with a couple of towels on full wash cycle at 40-50 degrees. Remove sock and allow felt to dry on the last. When dry on the outside remove from last and allow the felt to dry out completely.

Finishing boots and slippers

To prolong the life of felted footwear and prevent the wearer from slipping on smooth surfaces there are several methods of treating the soles.

1. Paint the sole with a latex solution which will provide a non-slip surface.
2. Cut a second sole from a firm piece of felt and machine stitch around this shape working from the edges inwards until the sole is covered with close lines of machine stitching which make the felt stronger. This outer sole can then be stitched to the base of the footwear and if wished can be coated with latex solution. An inner stitched sole can also be inserted into the footwear.
3. leather or suede can be cut to size and hand-stitched into position.
4. soles and heels can be added by a professional shoemaker.

Finishing the top edge is not essential but can add to the design of the footwear. Felt shapes can be appliquéd on around the edges to add extra strength and interest. A crocheted or knitted edging can be worked on to the felt.

Felt Hats

Traditional felt hats are made by blocking a seamless felt cone into the required shape. When the felt is dry it will retain the blocked shape. Cones are used to make small fairly close fitting hats such as pillbox styles which are worn on the back of the head or tilted forward over the brow, and cloches which fit closely to the head and come down over the ears. Capelines are larger and used to make hats with brims.

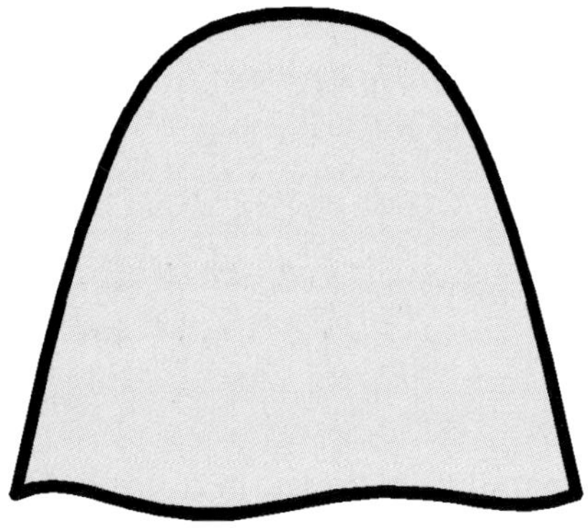

cone

capeline

The basic shape from which all the other patterns can be developed is the cone shape.

To make a pattern for a felt cone you require two measurements

a) the measurement around the head taken just above the eyebrows and the tops of the ears.

b) the measurement over the top of the head to half way down each ear.

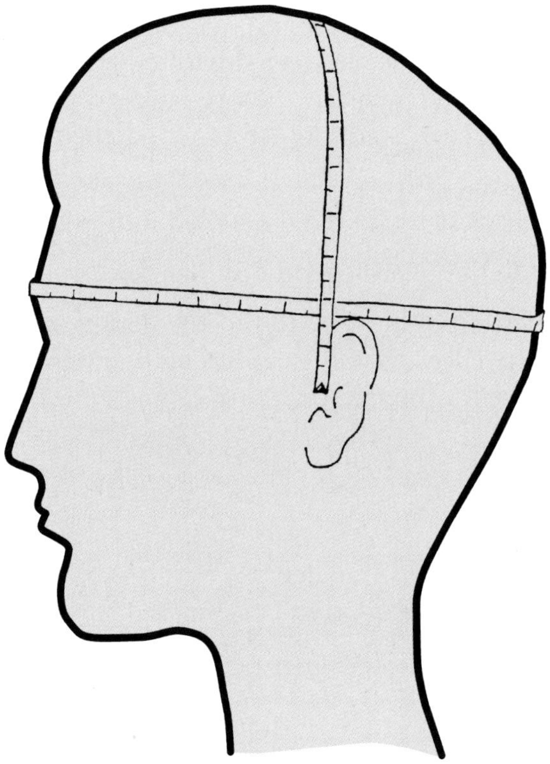

Calculating the pattern size for hand blocked felt hoods

To use these measurements to make a pattern it is necessary to divide each one in half and add 40% for shrinkage.

example : Measurement around head (a) $= \frac{56cm}{2} = 28cm = \frac{28 \times 4}{10} = 11.2$

$28 + 11.2 = 39.2$ *say 40 cm*

Measurement over top of head (b) $= \frac{36\ cm}{2} = 18\ cm = \frac{18 \times 4}{10} = 7.2\ cm$

$18 + 7.2 = 25.2$ *say 25 cm*

Use these measurements to draw a rectangle with (a) as the width and (b) as the height.
Mark in the centre point of the top line.
Draw in a curve for the crown of the hat by joining the lower corners of the rectangle with the centre top point - make sure this curve is not too shallow.
The basic rectangle can then be adapted to make the required shape for the different types of hat. See diagrams below :

Hat with brim

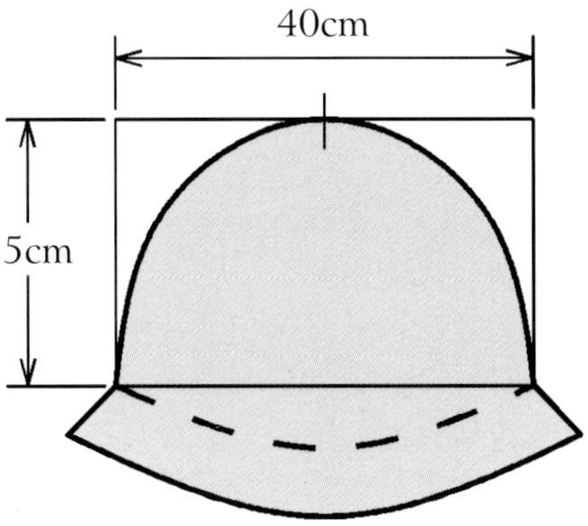

Cloche

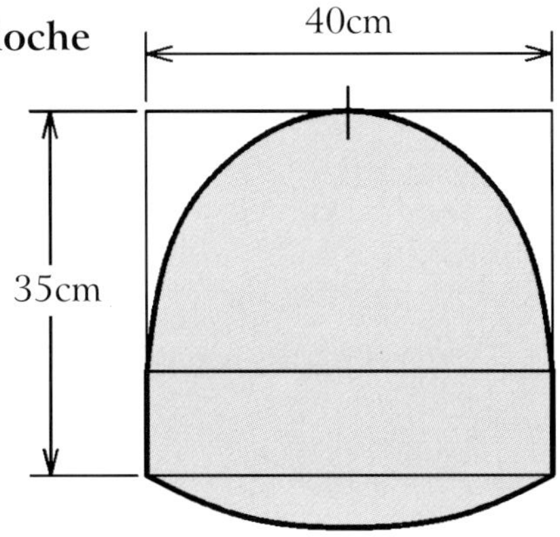

Pointed cone

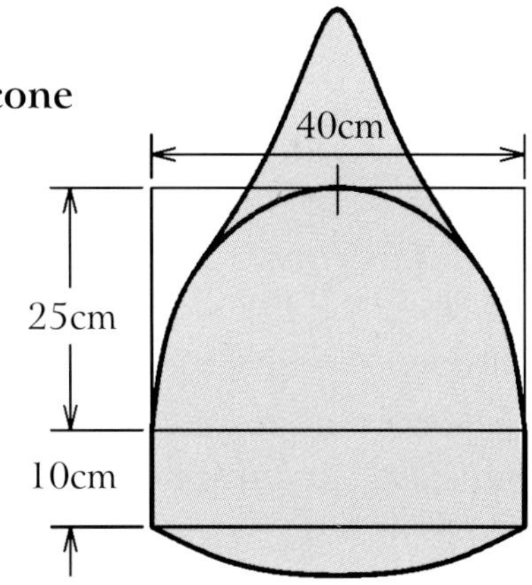

Felt hoods

Commercially felted cones are known in the hat trade as 'hoods' and ready made hoods can be bought from millinery suppliers. The price varies with the quality.

Template for felt cone

Once the shape and size has been calculated a paper pattern should then be made for the required size of cone. A template is cut in the same way as for the felt bag. But note that this time the pattern already includes the allowance for shrinkage so the template should be cut to the same size as the paper pattern.

To make felt cone

Follow steps 1 - 22 of method and instructions given for felt bag.
The main difference between making the cone and the bag is that it is important that the cone is kept even all the way around, and that attention is paid to avoiding thick ridges or weak spots which could cause problems when blocking the hat.

To avoid ridges
Place one hand inside the cone to support it and using a little soap to act as a lubricant carefully rub along the line where the fibres were folded over the edge of the template. If there is any sign of a ridge turn the cone carefully wrong side out and repeat the rubbing process.

To check for thin places
Hold cone up to the light and if any thin places are visible they should be treated to the rubbing treatment which shrinks the fibres and consequently the thin areas. Once any necessary 'First Aid' treatment has been administered then the hardening can be continued as for the bag but each time the cone is unfolded it should be rerolled with a different part at the edge to avoid forming a ridge.

If the lower edges of the cone begin to stretch out of shape with the rolling it is possible to shrink them by rolling only the lower part of the cone in the mat and continuing the felting process.

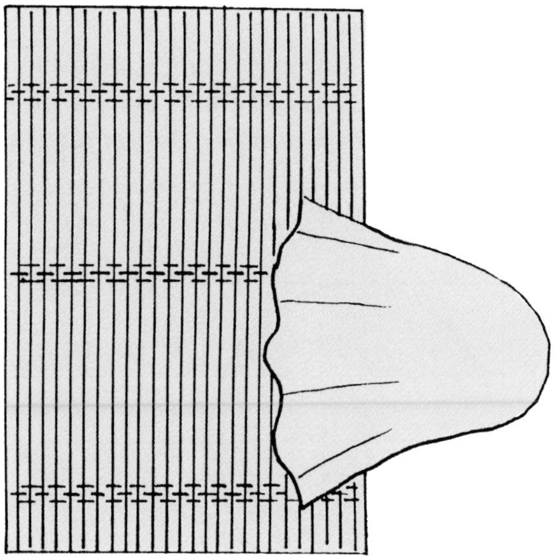

When the cone is well hardened and strong (see instructions for 3-dimensional bags) it is ready for shaping and blocking.

To block a felt cone:

1. First cover the hat block to be used with clingfilm. This will prevent the possible transference of dye from any previous hat.
2. Steam the felt cone by holding it over the spout of a boiling kettle. This will make the felt more elastic and will help it to stretch more easily.
3. Place the cone on to the hat block and firmly ease and stretch it downwards until it fits the block. If there is any fullness at the crown of the block this can be eased away by re-steaming the felt while on the block, and knocking the steam back into the felt using the side of the hand or by hammering the felt lightly with a rolling pin or wooden hammer. Pressing with a steam iron and damp cloth can also help remove unwanted fullness.
4. When the cone is stretched satisfactorily then hold in place with a piece of cord held with a slip knot, a piece of elastic or by pinning to the block with rust-proof drawing-pins. The depth of crown should be taken into consideration and the ties or drawing-pins should be just below the required depth. If the hat is to have a turned up brim it is useful to place something around the lower edge of the blocked crown so that the brim can be turned up over this while it dries. A padded roll can be made from cotton cloth bound with string or from plastic foam pipe-lagging which can be shaped to the right size and held in position with masking tape. Either of these methods will help to shape the brim and while it dries it will develop a curve rather than a fold.

6. When dry the hat may be left soft and unstiffened but if the design is a more formal one it is better to stiffen it so that it will hold its shape.

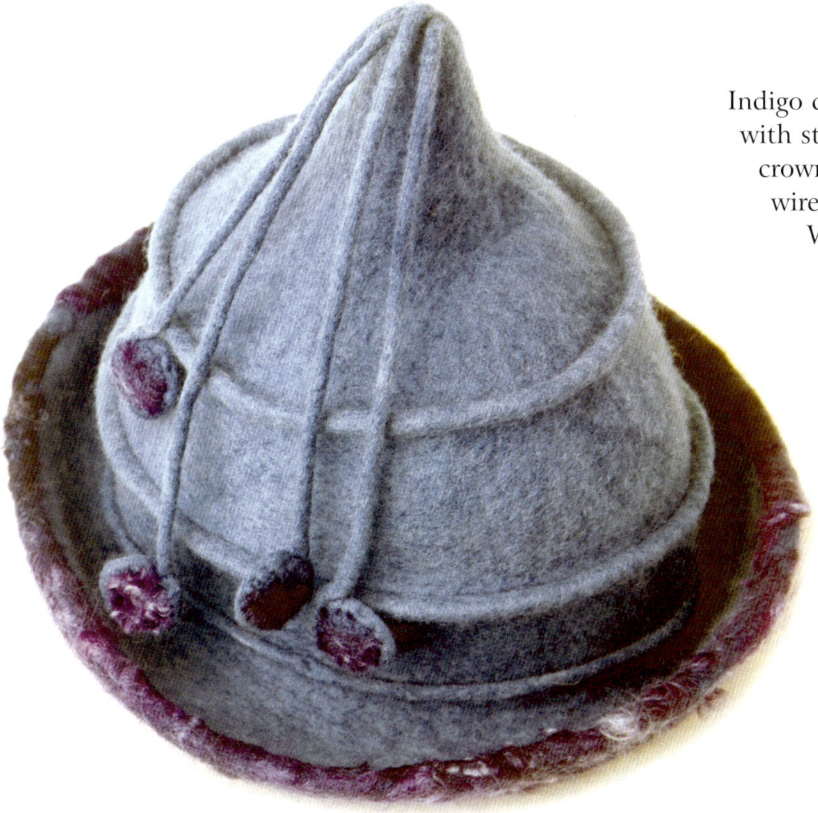

Indigo dyed merino felt hat with stitched tucks on the crown. The small upturned, wired brim is trimmed with Wensleydale fleece.

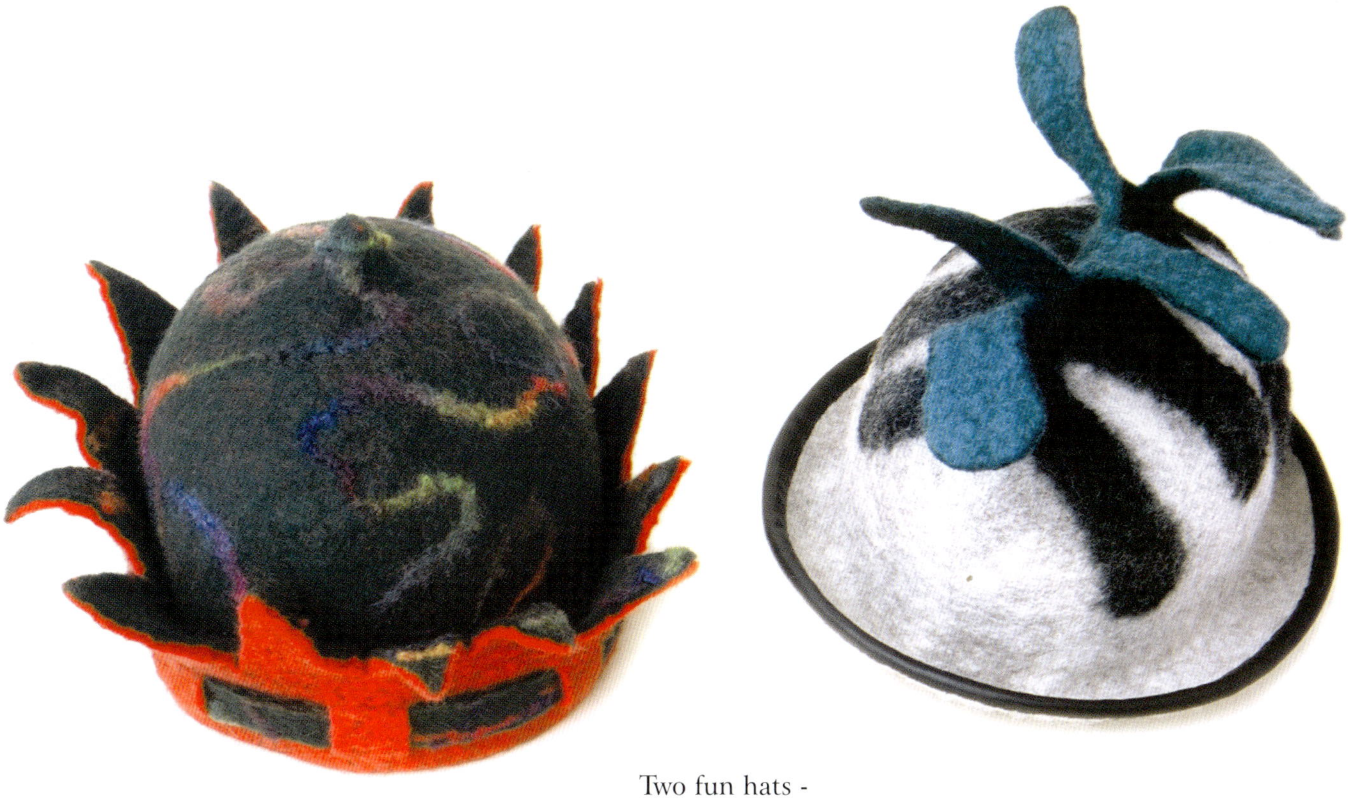

Two fun hats - 'Chicken Run' in grey Finn wool is trimmed with black and turquoise Merino and 'Hedgehog' in multi-coloured merino.

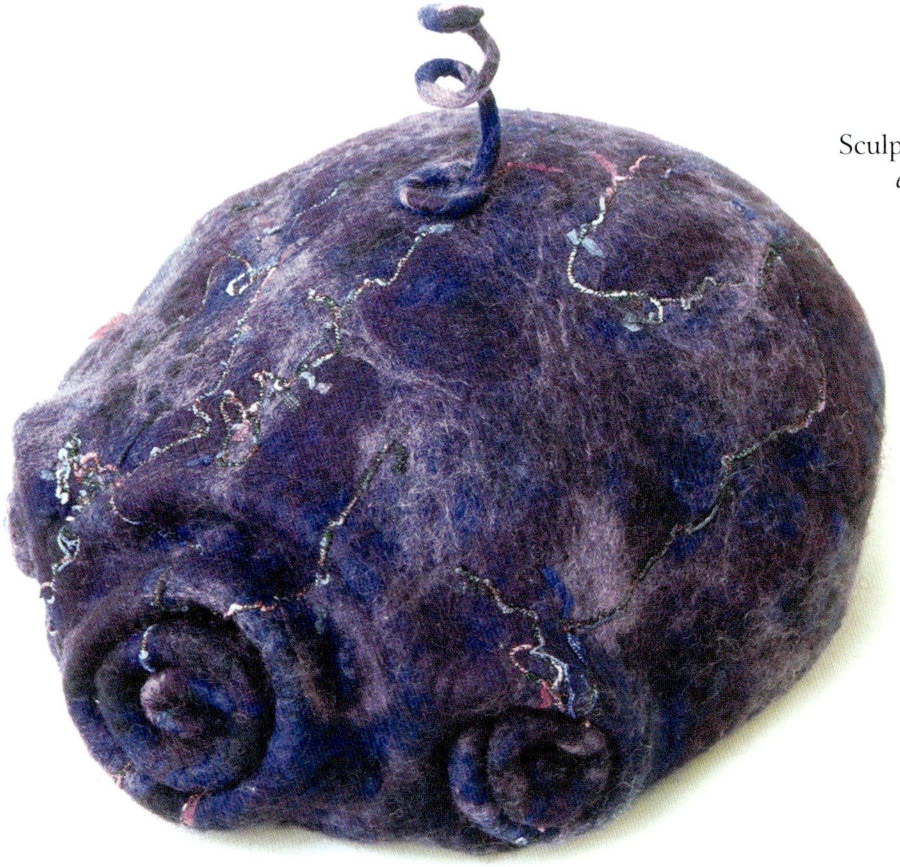

Sculpted beret - *a traditional beret shape extended and sculpted to produce a more sophisticated style.*

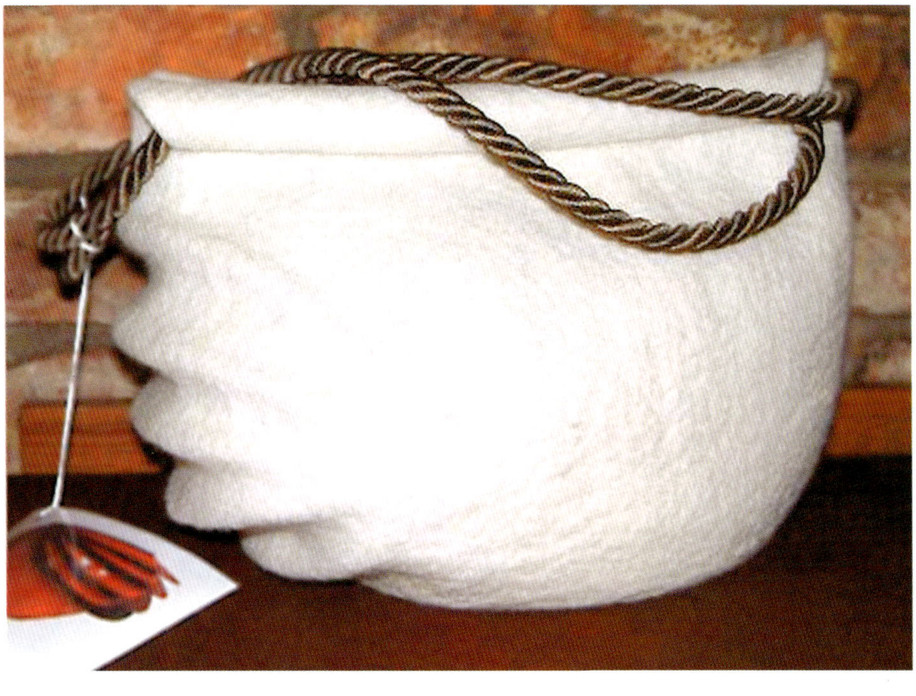

Natural white merino bag with interesting sculpted shapes made by Tessa Mendez.

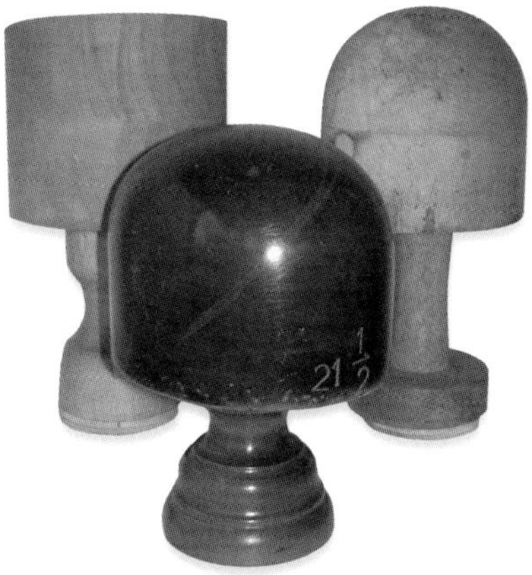

Hat Blocks
These are made from hardwood in different shapes and head sizes. The felt hood is steamed, stretched and dried on the block so that it takes its size and shape from the one being used. These blocks are hand made by specialist makers and are consequently expensive. The amateur hat maker can try blocking over a pudding bowl or other household container large enough for their head.

Felt Stiffener
There are two types of stiffener available on the market, one is a solvent which is applied to the inside of dry felt and the other a water based solution which can be applied to the wet felt. The solvent is applied as a light coating with a brush and allowed to dry. Great care must be taken when using solvent. It should be used sparingly and applied in a well ventilated area. The water based stiffener can also be applied with a brush or a spray but I find the most satisfactory method is to dilute the stiffener using 1 part stiffener to 3 parts water and immerse the wet felt in the solution. Squeeze out as much of the solution as possible, spin dry and then block the hat as usual. The diluted stiffener can be rebottled and used several times.

Finishing the Hat

Once the hat is blocked and dry it must be finished. The edge of the brim will need to be trimmed and finished off. If the hat is stiffened it is usual to wire the edge of the brim to hold it in shape. A headband made from petersham ribbon should also be stitched into the inside of the hat.

To wire a brim
Special millinery wire (see suppliers appendix) is used for this. It is available in different weights but the most frequently used size is no.6. The wire comes in a roll and must have excess spring removed from it before it is attached to the brim. To do this, first measure the length of wire required, cut off the length with wire cutters and then pull the wire through between thumb and forefinger while holding firmly and pulling against the curve.

A bound edge
1. Measure wire to fit the circumference of the brim plus approximately 5 cm for overlap.
2. Shape the wire into a circle and hold the overlap temporarily in position with a little fuse wire.
3. Stitch the wire to the edge of the brim with strong cotton and using wire stitch. Start stitching at the back of the hat just to the left of the join in the wire. Adjust the wire to fit the brim exactly and oversew the overlapping ends.
4. After wiring the edge can be bound with petersham ribbon.

A turned edge
If the edge of the brim is to be turned under instead of bound then the wire should be stitched to the underside of the brim about 1 cm in from the edge. After wiring, the edge of the brim can be folded under, pressed and machine stitched in position close to the edge of the wire. Finally any excess felt can be trimmed away close to the machine stitching.

Wire stitch

Begin by firmly over-sewing the wire to the edge of the brim two or three times. Working from right to left pass the thread over the wire and insert needle from back to front just under the wire and through the edge of the felt; pull the needle through and leave a loop of thread. Insert needle through the loop from the back to the front and pull thread up tight - this forms a small knot which lies on top of the wire and prevents the stitch from slipping. Repeat this around the brim. Stitches should be 13 - 19 mm apart ($^1/_2$ - $^3/_4$ inch).

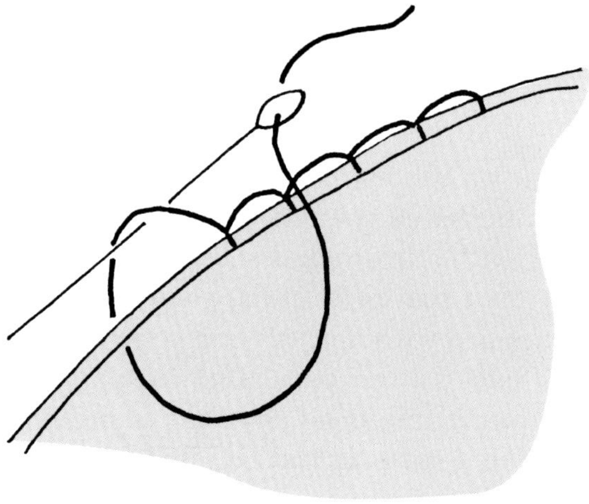

Headbands

A headband is a piece of petersham ribbon which is made to fit the size of the head and stitched into the inside of the lower edge of the crown. Cut off the required length of petersham ribbon which should be the head measurement plus 25mm for turnings. Steam press the ribbon and shape it into an arc by stretching one edge. Back stitch the two ends of the ribbon together and fit the headband into the hat with the larger stretched edge to the lower edge of the crown and working from the centre back. Fix in position with pins inserted vertically and then stitch in place using stab stitch. If the hat is slightly larger than the headband it should be eased evenly onto the band to make it fit. Finally complete the hat by adding the trimming to the outside.

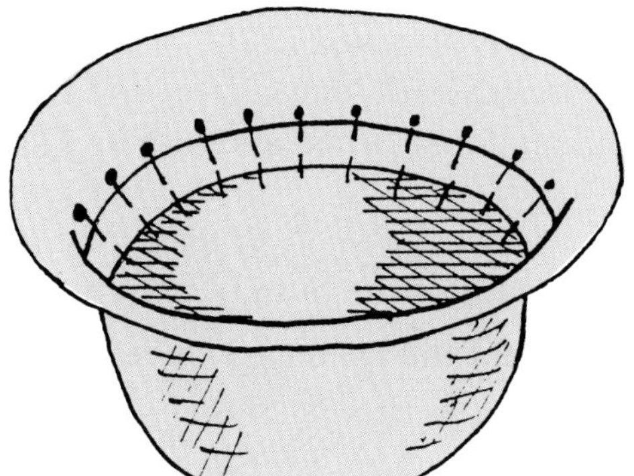

Sculpting Free Shapes

Virtually any free three dimensional shape can be made using the methods described throughout this booklet. If extensions and points are added to the original template innovative free shapes can be produced. These extensions can then be folded, pleated or twisted into the required positions. The hollow shape needs to be fairly well felted before the pleats or folds are put in place. The final shaping is achieved by rubbing the folds firmly with soapy water until they become firm and the required result is achieved. If necessary a few invisible hand-stitches can be inserted in the wrong side of the fold to stabilize it. Interesting hat shapes can be made in this way but free shaped vessels and containers and a wide variety of soft toys are also possible.

The diagram below shows the shape of the template used to make the sculpted beret *see the photographs of hats*. The template looks more suitable for the making of a octopus or jelly fish but the long points are folded in on themselves and pleated and sculpted to form the rosettes on the front of the beret. Points can extend from just one side or from several sides of a template - there are nor rules. Just have a go and have fun.

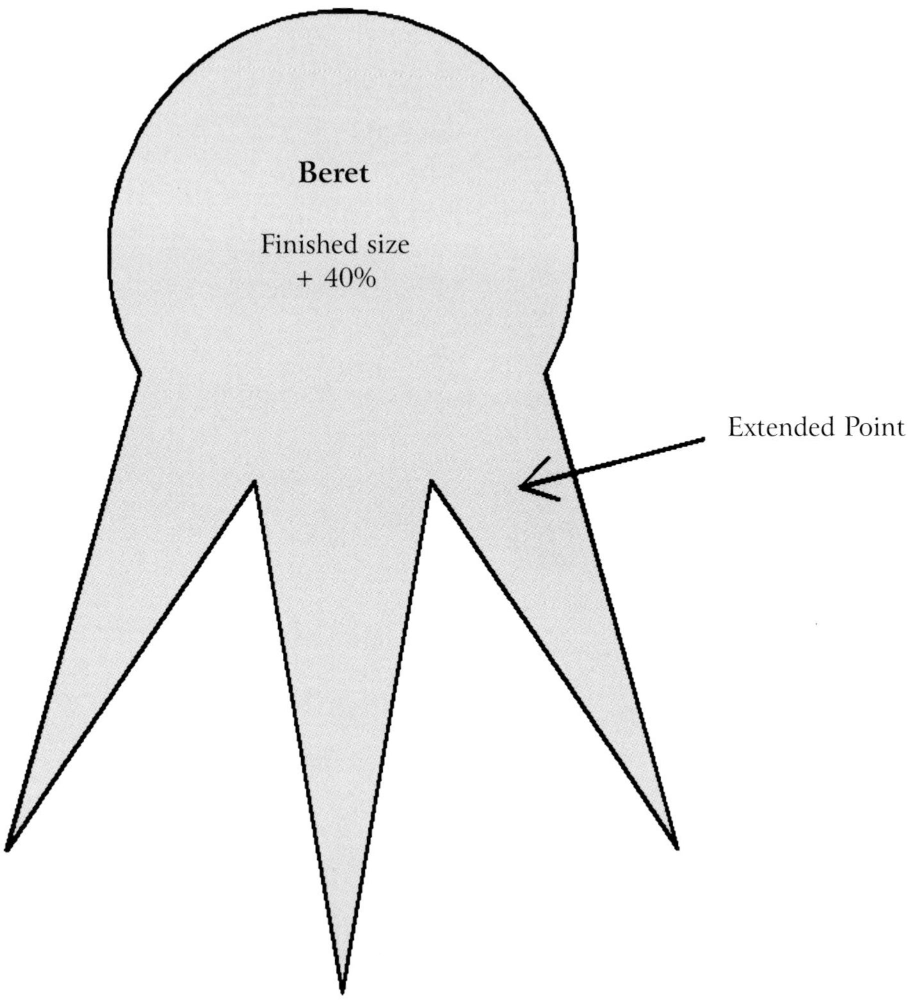

Suppliers

Adelaide Walker
2 Mill Yard Workshops
Wharfedale Business Centre
Otley Mills
Ilkley Road
Otley LS21 3JP
Tel : 01943 850812
Good range of fibres

Wingham Wool Work
70 Main Street
Wentworth
Rotherham
South Yorkshire
S62 7BR
Tel: 01226 742926
Fax: 01226 741166
Wide range of fibres and books

George Weil
Old Portsmouth Road
Peasmarsh
Guildford
Surrey
GU3 1LZ
Tel: 01483 565800
Fax: 01483 5
Fibres, dyes, books, informative catalogue

The Hat Trade
3 Neville Street
Tunbridge Wells
Kent
TR2 5RS
Tel: 01892 547847
millinery supplies

Boon and Lane
7-11 Taylor Street
Luton
Bedfordshire
Wooden hat blocks

Kartehuset
Ulla Winding
Vesterskovvej 8 DK - 5792
Aarslev
Denmark
Tel: + 45 65 99 1919
Fax: + 45 65 99 1981
Polystyrene shoe lasts, latex solution

Further Reading

Sjoberg, Gunilla Paetau — **Felt - New Directions for an ancient craft**
Translated by Patricia Spark,
Interweave Press Inc., 1996 ISBN 1-883010-17-9

Spark, Patricia — **Scandinavian Style Feltmaking**
Shuttlecraft Books, Couperville, Washington, 1992
ISBN 0-916658-50-3

Notes

Notes